MALICE
TOWARD
NONE

Abraham Lincoln's
SECOND INAUGURAL ADDRESS

Conceived and designed by
JACK E. LEVIN

Preface by
MARK R. LEVIN

THRESHOLD EDITIONS

NEW YORK LONDON TORONTO SYDNEY NEW DELHI

To my beautiful wife, Norma
Thank you for sixty-three years of wonderful marriage.

Threshold Editions
A Division of Simon & Schuster, Inc.
1230 Avenue of the Americas
New York, NY 10020

First Threshold Editions hardcover edition September 2014

THRESHOLD EDITIONS and colophon are trademarks of Simon & Schuster, Inc.

For information about special discounts for bulk purchases, please contact
Simon & Schuster Special Sales at 1-866-506-1949
or business@simonandschuster.com.

The Simon & Schuster Speakers Bureau can bring authors to your live event.
For more information or to book an event, contact the
Simon & Schuster Speakers Bureau at 1-866-248-3049
or visit our website at www.simonspeakers.com.

Jacket art and design by Alan Dingman

Manufactured in the United States of America

1   3   5   7   9   10   8   6   4   2

ISBN 978-1-4767-8426-7
ISBN 978-1-4767-8427-4 (ebook)

PREFACE

*L*ast year, on my visit to Florida to see my parents, Jack and Norma, I found my father spending a goodly amount of time working at his artist's easel. It is actually more like a well-worn easel desk. It is located toward the back of their modest but comfortable home in a tranquil area, where the sun shines most of the day and a light breeze can usually be felt through the screened porch. This is where my father has conceived and designed much of his artwork and books during his later years, including his beautiful editions *Abraham Lincoln's Gettysburg Address—Illustrated* and *George Washington—The Crossing*. It is also where he painted his magnificent portrait of President Ronald Reagan, which is displayed prominently today in the Ronald Reagan Library in Simi Valley, California.

As my father was leaning over his easel desk, surrounded by history books and with magazines and photographs at hand, maneuvering his X-ACTO knife across the desk with the exactitude of a surgeon, I asked him, "Dad, what are you working on?" "My next book," he said. I walked to where he was sitting and leaned over his shoulder. As he was diligently cutting and arranging lettering under a dramatic Civil War–era graphic, he began talking about the historical importance and modern-day relevance of Abraham Lincoln's second inaugural address. He explained that it was a seminal address intended to foster the national healing process and preach reconciliation as the devastation of America's most costly war was coming to an end. He reminded me that the celebrated phrase *"With malice toward none, with charity for all . . ."* was delivered by Lincoln at *that* speech, and Lincoln relied heavily on references to and inferences from faith and the Bible.

As my father explains and illustrates in his book, in myriad ways Lincoln's second inaugural address is considered his finest speech. Lincoln was enormously proud of it, although during the short time he remained alive after his second swearing-in he wondered how it would be accepted over the ages.

Just as the nation had tired of war, it had taken a heavy toll on Lincoln as well. After the address was delivered and Lincoln made his way back to the White House, Walt

Whitman, who observed the inauguration as one among the multitudes who crowded into Washington that day, reported: "I saw [Lincoln] on his return, at three o'clock, after the performance was over. He was in his plain two-horse barouche, and looked very much worn and tired; the lines, indeed, of vast responsibilities, intricate questions, and demands of life and death, cut deeper than ever upon his dark brown face; yet all the old goodness, tenderness, sadness, and canny shrewdness, underneath the furrows. (I never see that man without feeling that he is one to become personally attached to, for his combination of purest, heartiest tenderness, and native Western even rudest forms of manliness.) By his side sat his little boy, of ten years. There were no soldiers, only a lot of civilians on horseback, with huge yellow scarfs over their shoulders, riding around the carriage. . . ."*

Not until April 26, 1865, about seven weeks after Lincoln's March 4, 1865, second inaugural address, did the last of the Confederate forces finally surrender. The scale of the casualties and the scope of the destruction were inconceivable. My father reminds me that nearly *750,000* died during the Civil War, the equivalent of about *7,000,000* today.

*Walter Lowenfels, editor, *Walt Whitman's Civil War*, pp. 258–59

It is no accident that my father, a vigorous nearly ninety-year-old patriot born only sixty years after the end of the Civil War and a young volunteer when World War II broke out, is dedicated to highlighting some of America's most significant historical events and bringing them to life through his knowledge of the country's heritage and his creative artistic talents. As he mentioned to me several years ago, despite constant efforts to demean the remarkable qualities of our nation or ignore them altogether, his purpose in authoring his book series is to remind his fellow citizens, especially young people, how blessed we are to live in such a fantastic place. He has often said that this country is built on the unparalleled sacrifices, wisdom, courage, and spirit of the extraordinary men and women who came before us, both the prominent and the nameless. It is a profoundly distinctive legacy we must commemorate and preserve by passing it on to our children and grandchildren, just as it was passed on to us by our ancestors.

Malice Toward None—Abraham Lincoln's Second Inaugural Address is the latest volume in my father's trilogy of illustrated historical books. Why did he choose this subject? As he explained to me, "America faces many difficult and complicated challenges, both at home and abroad. Some days it may seem like the future is bleak or even hopeless. Now is a good time to remember that the nation's past is one of unthinkable and perilous trials, all of which we have surmounted. We are a people defined by amazing triumphs. No speech, and perhaps no occasion, better exemplifies this truth than Lincoln's second inaugural address."

My father never attempts or even presumes to improve upon the majestic words of a great statesman like Lincoln. Such a pursuit would be an egoist's folly. Instead, after the passing of 150 years, he sets the speech and surrounding events in a masterful visual display of period photographs and drawings, as if to bring history into the present and make it accessible to everyone. And I am proud to say he has outdone himself. *Malice Toward None—Abraham Lincoln's Second Inaugural Address* is an exquisite book.

Finally, there is no better place and time to mention my mother, Norma, about whom I am often asked. After all, she has always been the most loving and influential force behind the four men in our family. For my brothers, Doug and Robert, and for me, it is impossible to think of my father without thinking of my mother. Our parents have been married for more than sixty-three years and have been inseparable since they first met. They are real-life partners. They have always worked together and have never traveled apart. Alongside my father, my mother has worked very hard throughout her life—from starting and running a private nursery school and day camp and subsequently a small retail shop outside of Philadelphia. And no one has been more supportive of my father's creative and artistic endeavors than my mother. *Malice Toward None—Abraham Lincoln's Second Inaugural Address* and my father's other wonderful works would not have been possible without her encouragement.

I hope you enjoy the book. Share it with family and friends. And spread Abraham Lincoln's ageless message.

Mark R. Levin

FOREWORD

*I*n November 1864, Abraham Lincoln won a resounding electoral victory over Democrat George McClellan, whom he had removed a few years earlier as major general of the Union army. Although McClellan was popular with the troops, Lincoln lost trust in McClellan due to his indecisiveness and, at times, defiance. Lincoln's reelection, initially in some doubt, was improved significantly by a number of Union battlefield victories in the late summer of 1864, especially the Battle of Atlanta and the March to the Sea, led by Major General William Tecumseh Sherman.

On March 4, 1865, at his second inauguration, and on a day that began with miserable weather and heavy rain, Lincoln gave what many, including Lincoln himself, consider his greatest speech. Yes, even more profound than the Gettysburg Address. It was a speech delivered as the Civil War seemed to be coming to a close, with important victories in South and North Carolina, as well as Virginia, among other places. Indeed, thirty-six days later, Confederate general Robert E. Lee would surrender at the Appomattox Courthouse on April 9, 1865. Tragically, forty-one days after his second inauguration, Lincoln would be assassinated by John Wilkes Booth on April 14, 1865. Booth, along with other conspirators, was among the onlookers in the crowd that inauguration day.

Also present, and listening attentively to Lincoln's speech, was Frederick Douglass. The former slave was a courageous and outspoken leader of the abolitionist movement. Douglass was originally skeptical of Lincoln's commitment to ending slavery, but after their meetings and Lincoln's issuance of the Emancipation Proclamation on January 1, 1863, among other things, Douglass became an admirer. Douglass also attended the inaugural reception at the White House that evening, but was initially prevented from entering the East Room by policemen. He pushed his way past them and was quickly noticed by Lincoln. As Douglass recounted, Lincoln called out, "Here comes my friend Douglass." Lincoln shook Douglass's hand and said, "Douglass, I saw you in the crowd today listening to my inaugural address. There is no man's opinion that I value more than yours; what do you think of it?" Douglass replied, "Mr. Lincoln, it was a sacred effort."* It was the last time Douglass would see Lincoln.

And a sacred effort it was. On so many levels, Lincoln's Second Inaugural Address is among the most impressive of all speeches delivered by history's great statesmen. Although a mere 703 words and seven minutes in duration—not much longer than the 271-word Gettysburg Address and the second shortest inaugural speech of any president, bar George Washington's second inaugural speech—Lincoln could have claimed vindication or gloated about the Union's all but certain triumph, as so many political demagogues would have. In fact, the speech is devoid of the kind of endless personal references to "self" familiar in the prose of modern presidents. Nor did Lincoln set forth a long list of specific tasks confronting the nation and attempt to rally the people to their discharge, as many had expected. Instead, as at Gettysburg, Lincoln delivered the ideal speech. A speech where every word was carefully chosen, every sentence carefully structured. It was a *tour de force* not only in its precision but, more important, for its message of tolerance

---

*Allen Thorndike Rice, editor, *Reminiscences of Abraham Lincoln by Distinguished Men of His Time*, pp. 191–93

and reconciliation; its purpose was to address war-weary Americans and lay the foundation for peace.

Lincoln knew well that every corner of the country had been impacted by the war. The casualties were unimaginable, with hundreds of thousands dead. Postwar reconstruction would be an incredibly difficult and complex task involving the restoration of the economy, rebuilding cities and towns, assimilating regions, promoting racial harmony, caring for the maimed and widows, legal and constitutional challenges, and so much more. Although Lincoln would not live to lead the reconstruction efforts, the spirit and direction of his intentions could not have been clearer. They were best exemplified by these magnificent and most memorable words: *"With malice toward none, with charity for all . . ."*

During the course of the war, Lincoln was known to pray frequently, seeking strength from God and His hand in guidance. Some noted, including Douglass, that Lincoln's speech seemed fashioned after a sermon. In fact, nearly half the speech invokes references to God or scripture. Lincoln spoke of "the woe due to those by whom the offense [of slavery] came . . ." He observed that "Both [northerners and southerners] read the same Bible and pray to the same God, and each evokes His aid against the other. . . . The prayers of both could not be answered." Lincoln proclaimed that American slavery was a blight that God "now wills to remove" and, despite the toll in lives and treasure "the judgments of the Lord are true and righteous altogether." If there was ever any doubt that the Civil War was fought not only to maintain the Union but, in the end, to drive the horror of slavery from the land, there was no more.

It is reported by numerous reliable observers that when Lincoln began his second inaugural address, the stormy weather clouds of that day gave way to the light of a shining sun. It is an image that underscores Lincoln's exceptionality. He was not only an extraordinary president but a remarkable man whose wisdom will continue to span generations.

Jack E. Levin

Boynton Beach, Florida

At this second appearing to take the oath of the presidental office, there is less occasion for an extended address than there was
at the first.

Then a statement, somewhat in detail, of a course to be pursued, seemed fitting and proper.

A crowd gathers below the unfinished Capitol building for President Lincoln's first inauguration on March 4, 1861.

In your hands, my dissatisfied fellow countrymen, and not mine, is the momentous issue of Civil War. The Government will not assail you. You can have no conflict, without being yourselves the aggressors. You have no oath registered in Heaven to destroy the Government, while I shall have the most solemn one to preserve, protect, and defend it.

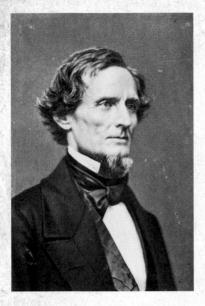

When Lincoln took his first-time oath as president of the United States, Jefferson Davis had already been elected president representing the states of the Confederacy: Alabama, South Carolina, Mississippi, Texas, Louisiana, and Florida. Lincoln tried as hard as he could to keep these states from seceding but failed because the real issue was that Republicans would not allow any additional slavery in any of the new states that were becoming a part of the United States.

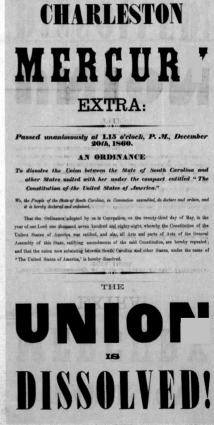

CHARLESTON

MERCURY

EXTRA:

Passed unanimously at 1.15 o'clock, P. M., December 20th, 1860.

AN ORDINANCE

To dissolve the Union between the State of South Carolina and other States united with her under the compact entitled "The Constitution of the United States of America."

We, the People of the State of South Carolina, in Convention assembled, do declare and ordain, and it is hereby declared and ordained,

That the Ordinance adopted by us in Convention, on the twenty-third day of May, in the year of our Lord one thousand seven hundred and eighty-eight, whereby the Constitution of the United States of America was ratified, and also, all Acts and parts of Acts of the General Assembly of this State, ratifying amendments of the said Constitution, are hereby repealed; and that the union now subsisting between South Carolina and other States, under the name of "The United States of America," is hereby dissolved.

THE

UNION

IS

DISSOLVED!

Now, at the expiration of four years, during which public declarations have been constantly called forth on every point and phase of the great contest which still absorbs the attention and engrosses the energies of the nation, little that is new could be presented.

The progress of our arms, upon which all else chiefly depends, is as well known to the public as to myself; and it is, I trust, reasonably satisfactory and encouraging to all.

With high hope for the future, no prediction in regard to it is ventured.

On the occasion corresponding to this four years ago all thoughts were anxiously directed to an impending civil war. All dreaded it— all sought to avert it.

Eleanor S. Brockenbrough Library, The Museum of the Confederacy, Richmond, VA

While the inaugural address was being delivered from this place, devoted altogether to *saving* the Union without war, insurgent agents were in the city seeking to *destroy* it without war—seeking to dissolve the Union, and divide effects, by negotiation. Both parties deprecated war; but one of them would *make* war rather than let the nation survive; and the other would *accept* war rather than let it perish.

Clement Laird Vallandigham was a politician, Ohio lawyer, and journalist who strongly opposed the war and tried, as a Democratic U.S. congressman, to obstruct war-related legistration. Lincoln banished him to the South after he was convicted of treason by a military commision in 1863. He was the acknowledged leader of the Copperheads, also known as the Peace Democrats. They persuaded the party to adopt a peace plank in the Democratic platform for the 1864 presidental election.

Confederate batteries fire on Fort Sumter on April 12, 1861, starting the Civil War.

THE SLAVE AUCTION.

One-eighth of the whole population were colored slaves, not distributed generally over the Union, but localized in the Southern part of it. These slaves constituted a peculiar and powerful interest. All knew that this interest was, somehow, the cause of the war.

To strengthen, perpetuate, and extend this interest was the object for which the insurgents would rend the Union, even by war; while the government claimed no right to do more than to restrict the territorial enlargement of it.

Neither party expected for the war the magnitude or the duration which it has already attained.

Lincoln presenting his very important document to his cabinet for the first time, July 22, 1862.

Neither anticipated that the *cause* of the conflict might cease with or even before the conflict itself should cease.

BY THE PRESIDENT OF THE UNITED STATES OF AMERICA.

A Proclamation.

Whereas, on the twenty-second day of September, in the year of our Lord one thousand eight hundred and sixty-two, a proclamation was issued by the President of the United States, containing, among other things, the following, to wit:

"That on the first day of January, in the year of our Lord one thousand eight hundred and sixty-three, all persons held as slaves within any State or designated part of a State, the people whereof shall then be in rebellion against the United States, shall be then, thenceforward, and forever, free; and the Executive government of the United States, including the military and naval authority thereof, will recognize and maintain the freedom of such persons, and will do no act or acts to repress such persons, or any of them, in any efforts they may make for their actual freedom.

"That the Executive will, on the first day of January aforesaid, by proclamation, designate the States and parts of States, if any, in which the people thereof, respectively, shall then be in rebellion against the United States; and the fact that any State, or the people thereof, shall on that day be in good faith represented in the Congress of the United States, by members chosen thereto at elections wherein a majority of the qualified voters of such State shall have participated, shall, in the absence of strong countervailing testimony, be deemed conclusive evidence that such State, and the people thereof, are not then in rebellion against the United States."

Now, therefore, I, ABRAHAM LINCOLN, PRESIDENT OF THE UNITED STATES, by virtue of the power in me vested as commander-in-chief of the army and navy of the United States, in time of actual armed rebellion against the authority and government of the United States, and as a fit and necessary war measure for suppressing said rebellion, do, on this first day of January, in the year of our Lord one thousand eight hundred and sixty-three, and in accordance with my purpose so to do, publicly proclaimed for the full period of one hundred days from the day first above mentioned, order and designate as the States and parts of States wherein the people thereof, respectively, are this day in rebellion against the United States, the following, to wit: ARKANSAS, TEXAS, LOUISIANA, (except the Parishes of St. Bernard, Plaquemines, Jefferson, St. John, St. Charles, St. James, Ascension, Assumption, Terre Bonne, Lafourche, St. Mary, St. Martin, and Orleans, including the City of New Orleans), MISSISSIPPI, ALABAMA, FLORIDA, GEORGIA, SOUTH CAROLINA, NORTH CAROLINA, and VIRGINIA, (except the forty-eight counties designated as West Virginia, and also the counties of Berkeley, Accomac, Northampton, Elizabeth City, York, Princess Ann, and Norfolk, including the cities of Norfolk and Portsmouth,) and which excepted parts are for the present left precisely as if this proclamation were not issued.

And by virtue of the power and for the purpose aforesaid, I do order and declare that all persons held as slaves within said designated States and parts of States are and henceforward shall be free; and that the Executive government of the United States, including the military and naval authorities thereof, will recognize and maintain the freedom of said persons.

And I hereby enjoin upon the people so declared to be free to abstain from all violence, unless in necessary self-defence; and I recommend to them that, in all cases when allowed, they labor faithfully for reasonable wages.

And I further declare and make known that such persons, of suitable condition, will be received into the armed service of the United States, to garrison forts, positions, stations, and other places, and to man vessels of all sorts in said service.

And upon this act, sincerely believed to be an act of justice warranted by the Constitution upon military necessity, I invoke the considerate judgment of mankind and the gracious favor of Almighty God.

In witness whereof I have hereunto set my hand and caused the seal of the United States to be affixed.

[L. S.] Done at the CITY OF WASHINGTON this first day of January, in the year of our Lord one thousand eight hundred and sixty-three, and of the Independence of the United States of America the eighty-seventh.

By the President: *Abraham Lincoln*

William H. Seward, Secretary of State.

A true copy, with the autograph signatures of the President and the Secretary of State.

Jno. G. Nicolay, Priv. Sec. to the President.

The Emancipation Proclamation

Each looked for an easier triumph, and
a result less fundamental and astounding.

Both read the same Bible,
and pray to the same God;

and each invokes
His aid against the other.

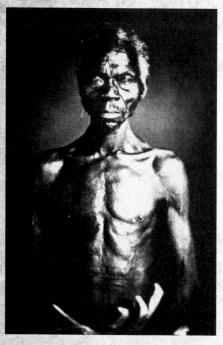

It may seem strange that any men should dare to ask a just God's assistance in wringing their bread from the sweat of other men's faces, but let us judge not that we be not judged.

The prayers of both could not be answered—that of neither has been answered fully. The Almighty has His own purposes. "Woe unto the world because of offences! for it must needs be that offences come, but woe to that man by whom the offence cometh."

If we shall suppose that American slavery is one of those offences which, in the providence of God, must needs come, but
which, having continued through His appointed time, He now
wills to remove, and that He gives to both the North and the
South this terrible war, as the woe due to those by whom the

offence came, shall we discern therein any departure from those divine attributes which the believers in a living God always ascribe to Him? Fondly do we hope—fervently do we pray—that this mighty scourge of war may speedily pass away.

Yet, if God wills that it continue until all the wealth piled by the bondman's two hundred and fifty years of unrequited toil shall be sunk, and until every drop of blood drawn with the lash shall be paid by another drawn with the sword, as was said three thousand years ago so still it must be said, "The judgments of the Lord are true and righteous altogether."

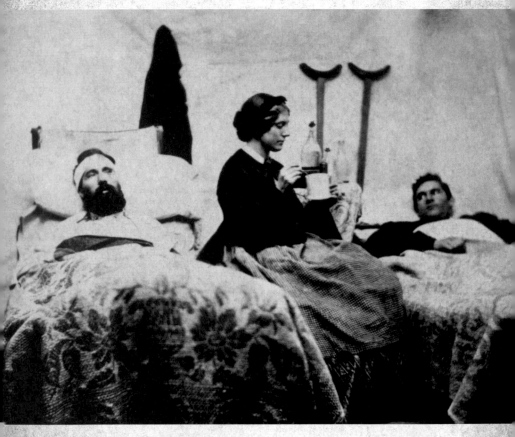

With malice toward none; with charity for all; with firmness in the right, as God gives us to see the right, let us strive on to finish the work we are in; to bind up the nation's wounds; to care for him who shall have borne the battle, and for his widow, and his orphan—to do all which may achieve and cherish a just and lasting peace, among ourselves, and with all nations.

facing page: Confederate General Stonewall Jackson's widow and child. His last words to her as he died were, "Let us cross over the river and rest under the shade of the trees."

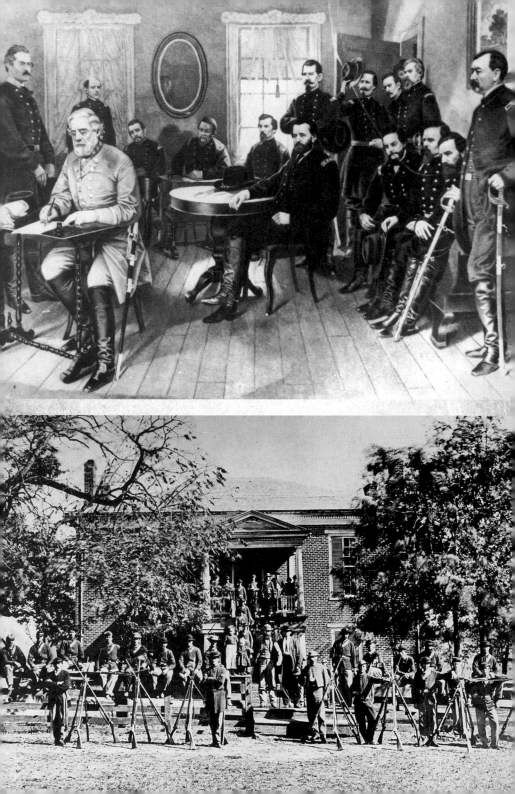

Union General Ulysses S. Grant.

Confederate General Robert E. Lee.

UNION

VICTORY!

PEACE!

Surrender of General Lee and His Whole Army.

facing page: McLean home at Appomattox Court House, Virginia, in whose parlor General Lee surrendered to General Grant, bringing the Civil War to an end, April 9, 1865.

In 1913 the government held a fiftieth anniversary reunion at Gettysburg battlefield. Fifty thousand survivors of both North and South attended in brotherhood and friendship, thanks in part to the memory and prayers of Abraham Lincoln.

"The Blue and the Gray at Gettysburg, Assembly Tent" (fiftieth-anniversary reunion, Gettysburg, Pennsylvania, 1913).

Cover of *Blue and Gray* magazine, March 1893.

My Comrades of the Confederate Army, my friends and veterans of the Federal Army . . . I am filled with emotion as I look upon survivors of the armies of the Civil War and remember that here, at Gettysburg, was fought one of the greatest and most decisive battles of the Civil War. We are not here with battle flags, charging brigades, roaring cannon, rattling musketry, and dead and dying soldiers, but we are here with friendship and fraternity, good will and glorious peace. A half century has made those who wore the Blue and those who wore the Gray stand together as friends, and behold the Bow of Peace and promise in the sky, and look with pleasure upon the flag of our country, as it presents the stars of Re-United States and represents reunited people. . . . While those of us who were soldiers when the battle of Gettysburg was fought will always remember the glory and the gloom of that period, we may well thank God, today, that the benediction of peace and reconciliation spreads over our great Republic, and we realize that the immortal words now most conspicuous are, "One country, one constitution, one flag, and one destiny."

—James B. McCreary, governor of Kentucky,
remarks at the Gettysburg Reunion, 1913

Fellow Countrymen:

At this second appearing to take the oath of the presidential office there is less occasion for an extended address than there was at the first. Then a statement, somewhat in detail, of a course to be pursued, seemed fitting and proper. Now, at the expiration of four years, during which public declarations have been constantly called forth on every point and phase of the great contest which still absorbs the attention, and engrosses the energies of the nation, little that is new could be presented. The progress of our arms, upon which all else chiefly depends, is as well known to the public as to myself, and it is, I trust, reasonably satisfactory and encouraging to all. With high hope for the future, no prediction in regard to it is ventured.

On the occasion corresponding to this four years ago, all thoughts were anxiously directed to an impending civil war. All dreaded it—all sought to avert it. While the inaugural address was being delivered from this place, devoted altogether to saving the Union without war, insurgent agents were in

the city seeking to destroy it without war—seeking to dissolve the Union, and divide effects, by negotiation. Both parties deprecated war; but one of them would make war rather than let the nation survive; and the other would accept war rather than let it perish. And the war came.

One eighth of the whole population were colored slaves, not distributed generally over the Union, but localized in the Southern part of it. These slaves constituted a peculiar and powerful interest. All knew that this interest was, somehow, the cause of the war. To strengthen, perpetuate, and extend this interest was the object for which the insurgents would rend the Union, even by war; while the government claimed no right to do more than to restrict the territorial enlargement of it. Neither party expected for the war, the magnitude, or the duration, which it has already attained. Neither anticipated that

The Second Inaugural Address in Abraham Lincoln's own handwriting. It covered only four pages of copy paper.

the causes of the conflict might cease with, or
even before, the conflict itself should cease, Each
looked for an easier triumph, and a result less
fundamental and astounding. Both read the same
Bible, and pray to the same God; and each invokes His aid against the other. It may seem
strange that any men should dare to ask a just
God's assistance in wringing their bread from
the sweat of other men's faces; but let us judge
not that we be not judged. The prayers of
both could not be answered; that of neither
has been answered fully. The Almighty has His
own purposes. "Woe unto the world because
of offences! for it must needs be that offences come; but woe to that man by whom
the offence cometh!" If we shall suppose
that American Slavery is one of those offences
which, in the providence of God, must needs
come, but which, having continued through
His appointed time, He now wills to remove,
and that He gives to both North and South,
this terrible war, as the woe due to those

by whom the offence came, shall we discern there
in any departure from those divine attributes
which the believers in a Living God always
ascribe to Him? Fondly do we hope, fervently do we pray, that this mighty scourge of
war may speedily pass away. Yet, if God
wills that it continue, until all the wealth
piled by the bond-man's two hundred and
fifty years of unrequited toil shall be sunk,
and until every drop of blood drawn with the
lash, shall be paid by another drawn with
the sword, as was said three thousand years
ago, so still it must be said "the judgments
of the Lord, are true and righteous altogether"

With malice toward none;
with charity for all; with firmness in the
right, as God gives us to see the right,
let us strive on to finish the work we
are in; to bind up the nation's wounds;
to care for him who shall have borne the battle, and for his widow, and his orphan—
to do all which may achieve and cherish a just
and a lasting peace, among ourselves, and with all nations.

Lincoln did not read the address from this handwritten copy
but from a printed galley of two columns.

Fellow-Countrymen:

At this second appearing to take the oath of the presidential office, there is less occasion for an extended address than there was at the first. Then a statement, somewhat in detail, of a course to be pursued, seemed fitting and proper. Now, at the expiration of four years, during which public declarations have been constantly called forth on every point and phase of the great contest which still absorbs the attention and engrosses the energies of the nation, little that is new could be presented. The progress of our arms, upon which all else chiefly depends, is as well known to the public as to myself; and it is, I trust, reasonably satisfactory and encouraging to all. With high hope for the future, no prediction in regard to it is ventured.

On the occasion corresponding to this four years ago, all thoughts were anxiously directed to an impending civil war. All dreaded it—all sought to avert it. While the inaugural [sic] address was being delivered from this place, devoted altogether to *saving* the Union without war, insurgent agents were in the city seeking to *destroy* it without war—seeking to dissolve the Union, and divide effects, by negotiation. Both parties deprecated war; but one of them would *make* war rather than let the nation survive; and the other would *accept* war rather than let it perish. And the war came.

One-eighth of the whole population were colored slaves, not distributed generally over the Union, but localized in the Southern part of it. These slaves constituted a peculiar and powerful interest. All knew that this interest was, somehow, the cause of the war. To strengthen, perpetuate, and extend this interest was the object for which the insurgents would rend the Union, even by war; while the government claimed no right to do more than to restrict the territorial enlargement of it. Neither party expected for the war the magnitude, or the duration, which it has already attained. Neither anticipated that the *cause* of the conflict might cease with, or even before, the conflict itself should cease. Each looked for an easier triumph, and a result less fundamental and astounding. Both read the same Bible, and pray to the same God; and each invokes His aid against the other. It may seem strange that any men should dare to ask a just God's assistance in wringing their bread from the sweat of other men's faces; but let us judge not, that we be not judged. The prayers of both could not be answered—that of neither has been answered fully. The Almighty has his own purposes. "Woe unto the world because of offences! for it must needs be that offences come; but woe to that man by whom the offence cometh!" If we shall suppose that American slavery is one of those offences which, in the providence of God, must needs come, but which, having continued through His appointed time, He now wills to remove, and that He gives to both North and South, this terrible war, as the woe due to those by whom the offence came, shall we discern therein any departure from those divine attributes which the believers in a Living God always ascribe to Him? Fondly do we hope—fervently do we pray—that this mighty scourge of war may speedily pass away. Yet, if God wills that it continue, until all the wealth piled by the bondman's two hundred and fifty years of unrequited toil shall be sunk, and until every drop of blood drawn with the lash shall be paid by another drawn with the sword, as was said three thousand years ago, so still it must be said, "The judgments of the Lord are true and righteous altogether."

With malice toward none; with charity for all; with firmness in the right, as God gives us to see the right, let us strive on to finish the work we are in; to bind up the nation's wounds; to care for him who shall have borne the battle, and for his widow, and his orphan—to do all which may achieve and cherish a just and lasting peace, among ourselves, and with all nations.

facing page: Visitors to the Lincoln Memorial on the Mall in Washington, D.C., see two of Abraham Lincoln's magnificent speeches carved in full—the Gettysburg Address and the Second Inaugural Address.

PICTURE CREDITS